Bubby's Guide

to
Traditional
Passover
Cooking

A Grandma's Guide
to a Perfect Passover

Bubby's Guide™ is a trademark of Rite Lite Ltd.

Rite Lite Ltd, Publisher

Brooklyn NY

First Edition

Published by:
Rite Lite Ltd.
333 Stanley Avenue
Brooklyn NY 11207
www.riteliteltd.com

Designed and edited by Jennifer Twersky
Printed in China

ISBN: 0-9772560-0-6

Library of Congress Control Number: 2005908390

Foreword

Hello and welcome! I hope you find this guide useful and enjoyable! I feel that I should tell you that the idea for this cookbook did not come from me. I *generally* mind my own business and *rarely* offer my advice, on *any* subject. However, my children and grandchildren pointed out the opportunity to help out. There are many people out there who would like to try their hand at preparing their own Seder and Passover meals. They find the idea daunting, yet...somehow appealing.

Well, I know I can help. I was raised in a very traditional prewar European home where I absorbed all of the important basics of traditional holiday cooking (and Passover is the **Big One**). After fleeing the Holocaust with my husband and reestablishing my family here in America (New York to be precise) I continued to perfect my cooking skills while raising my family.

Well, it's over a half-century of Passovers later, and I've been blessed with children, grandchildren and great-grandchildren who join our Seder. I can tell you - if you have some help, and are willing to try, it's really not that big a deal!

With this handy guide, it's my pleasure to help you embark on the adventure of traditional Passover cooking. Jennifer did a superb job of bringing all the recipes and instructions together in a concise and easy-to-use format. I know you'll do fine. Remember, Bubby knows best!

Love,

Bubby (a.k.a. Grandma)

P.S. Just to share an extra tip with you, I was taught early on to only invite as many people as you have settings for. Thought you'd like that one!

Table of Contents

First Seder

Appetizer
Stuffed Cabbage (page 20)

Soup
Traditional Chicken Soup with Fluffy Matzah Balls
(page 31, 34)

Entrees
Sweet and Sour Pot Roast (page 69)
Chickens in Apricot Sauce (page 63)
Red Snapper (page 49)

Side Dishes
Potato Kugel (page 89)
Zucchini Pudding (page 84)

Desserts
Chocolate Almond Cake (page 96)
Lemon Sponge Cake (page 103)
Cranberry Apple Crisp (page 97)

Second Seder

Appetizer
Traditional Gefilte Fish (page 47)

Soup
Chicken Beef Soup (page 32)

Entrees
Veal Brisket (page 73)
Chicken Sauté with Potatoes (page 64)
Pickled Salmon (page 44)

Side Dishes
Matzah Stuffing (page 87)
Squash Pudding (page 81)

Desserts
Divine Chocolate Cake (page 102)
Scrumptious Nut Cake (page 99)
Pineapple Sorbet (page 107)

Dairy Lunch

Appetizer
Eggplant Salad (page 23)

Soup
Tasty Tomato Soup (page 38)

Entrees
Matzah Lasagna (page 53)
Cheese Blintzes (page 54)
Yemenite Fish (page 46)

Side Dishes
Broccoli Walnut Ring (page 80)
Garlic "Bread" (page 78)

Desserts
Fabulous Cheesecake (page 108)
Strawberry Shortcake (page 95)
Ice Cream Puffs (page 109)

Formal Lunch

Appetizer
Creamy Potato Salad (page 26)

Soup
Chilled Cherry Soup (page 39)

Entrees
Brisket of Beef (page 68)
Chicken a La King (page 66)
Festive Fish (page 43)

Side Dishes
Pareve "Noodle" Kugel (page 88)
Carrot Tzimmes (page 91)
Cholent (page 71)

Desserts
Chocolate Carrot Cake (page 98)
Seven Layer Cake (page 101)
Almond Macaroons (page 104)

Formal Dinner

Appetizer
Sunny Salad (page 22)

Soup
Traditional Cabbage Soup (page 36)

Entrees
Mouth Watering Meatballs (page 67)
Turkey with Spice (page 70)
Spinach Stuffed Fillets (page 48)

Side Dishes
Colorful Peppers (page 83)
Potato Kugel (page 89)

Desserts
Blondies (page 106)
Chocolate Mousse Torte (page 100)
Pineapple Sorbet (page 107)

The Seder

The Seder

The Seder

The word **"Seder"** means **"order."** The Seder service has 14 parts that are performed in sequence. Some people sing the names of the parts of the Seder service, stopping on the second time through, at the part they are about to begin. The **14** parts are as follows:

1. **KADESH** - *Sanctify:* The Seder service begins with the recitation of Kiddush, the Blessing proclaiming the sanctity of the Holiday over a cup of wine, the first of the Four Cups.

2. **URCHATZ** - *Wash Hands:* We wash our hands in the ritual manner as before a meal, but without the customary blessing.

3. **KARPAS** - *The Vegetable:* A small piece of parsley, boiled potato, or other vegetable, is dipped into salt water and eaten.

4. **YACHATZ** - *Divide (the Matzah):* The middle Matzah is broken in two. The larger part is put aside for later use as the Afikomen.

5. **MAGGID** - *Tell the Story:* The story of the Exodus from Egypt is read out loud from the special Haggadah book. This is followed by the second cup of wine.

6. **RACHTZAH** - *Wash Hands Before the Meal:* The hands are washed again, this time with the customary blessing, as is usually done before eating bread.

7. **MOTZI MATZAH** - *Eating the Matzah.*

8. **MAROR** - *Bitter Herb:* The bitter herb is dipped in the Charoset and eaten.

9. **KORECH** - *Sandwich:* Eat a sandwich of Matzah and Maror.

10. **SHULCHAN ORECH** - *The Holiday Meal.*

11. **TZAFUN** - *The Afikomen:* After the meal, the half matzah which had been set aside for the Afikomen, is taken out and eaten.

12. **BARECH** - *Grace after the Meal:* This is followed by the third cup of wine. Fill the Elijah Cup, open the door and recite the passage inviting the Prophet Elijah.

13. **HALLEL** - *Songs of Praise:* These are sung followed by the fourth cup of wine.

14. **NIRTZAH** - *The Conclusion of the Seder:* We say/sing additional prayers concluding with "Chad Gadya."

Having carried out the Seder service properly, we are sure that it has been well received by G-d. We then say "L'Shanah Haba'ah b'Yerushalyim -- Next year in Jerusalem."

On the Passover Table

1. **SEDER PLATE** - see page 11 for details.

2. **THREE MATZAHS** - in a sectioned matzah cover or on the Seder Plate covered with a large napkin.

3. **WINE CUPS** - one for each individual present - used to drink the Four Cups of wine.

4. **ELIJAH CUP** - a special wine cup filled as a symbolic hope for the coming of the Messiah.

5. **SALT WATER** - symbolic of the tears shed by the Jews in Egypt.

6. **HAGGADAH -** the ritual book used during the Seder to relate the story of the Exodus from Egypt.

The Seder Plate

It is a good idea to prepare the Seder Table long before the Seder meal so you aren't pressured to get it ready at the last minute. It allows time to reflect on the symbolism of the foods and connect to the Passover story.

The **K'ARAH** *(Seder plate)* is where the ceremonial foods are arranged. It consists of the following:

1. **Z'ROAH** - *Arm:* a shank bone dry roasted over an open flame. This symbolizes the "Mighty Arm of G-d". It also represents the Paschal lamb offered as the Passover sacrifice in the Great Temple. To prepare, broil a koshered lamb shank (or alternatively, a chicken neck) over a flame until it is brown and tender.

2. **BEITZA** - *Egg:* a hard-boiled egg browned slightly over an open flame. This represents the offering brought in the Temple on Festivals.

3. **MAROR** - *Bitter Herb:* romaine lettuce or grated horseradish. These symbolize the bitter life of the Jews enslaved in Egypt. The Maror is dipped in the Charoset before being eaten. To prepare fresh horseradish, scrape the root clean, then grate or slice it. To prepare romaine lettuce, select leaves from the head of the lettuce and wash well.

4. **CHAROSET** - *Mixture of nuts, apples, and wine:* which symbolizes the mortar used in making bricks for Pharoah. (Recipes for this are found on pages 13-16.)

5. **KARPAS** - *Vegetable:* usually parsley or cooked potato (alternatively, parsnip, radish, onion, or celery), which symbolizes the meager diet of the Jews bondage. The Karpas is dipped in salt water before eating.

6. **CHAZERET** - *Sprouted Horseradish Head:* which is a symbol of spring.

Traditional Charoset

Ingredients:

2 **bananas**, peeled and chopped
2 **apples**, cored, peeled and chopped
Juice and grated zest of ½ **lemon**
Juice and grated zest of ½ **orange**
½ cup **pistachios**, ground
15 pitted **dates**, chopped
1 teaspoon ground **cinnamon**
¼ cup sweet **wine**
5 tablespoons **matzah meal**

Preparation:

Combine bananas, apples, lemon juice, lemon zest, orange juice, orange zest, nuts, and dates in large bowl; **mix** well. Add cinnamon, wine and matzah meal; **blend** thoroughly. Chill.

Yemenite Charoset

Ingredients:

15 pitted **dates**, chopped
15 dried **figs**, chopped
2 tablespoons **sesame seeds** (optional)
1 teaspoon ground **ginger**
Dash of ground **coriander**
Red wine
1 small **chili pepper** or pinch of **cayenne pepper** (optional)

Preparation:

Combine & mix to create a **thick** paste. Yields about **2½ cups.**

Persian Charoset

Ingredients:
1 **apple**, cored and grated
8-10 pitted **dates**, chopped
¼ cup **almonds**, ground
¼ cup **pistachio** or **pine nuts**, ground
¼ cup **raisins**
Juice and rind of **lemon**
½ teaspoon **cinnamon**
Sweet **red wine**

Preparation:
Combine all ingredients, adding enough wine to create a **paste**.

Turkish Charoset

Ingredients:
½ cup pitted **dates**, finely chopped
½ cup **figs**, finely chopped
½ cup dried **apricots**, finely chopped
½ cup **almonds** or **walnuts**, finely chopped
1 **apple**, peeled, cored and grated

Preparation:
Combine all ingredients, adding enough wine to create a **paste**.

Greek Charoset

Ingredients:
½ cup **black currants**, finely chopped
½ cup **raisins**, finely chopped
½ cup **almonds** or **pine nuts**, finely chopped
½ cup **dates**, finely chopped
2 tablespoons **honey** (optional)
Sweet **red wine**

Preparation:
Combine all ingredients, adding enough wine to create a **paste**.

Israeli Charoset

Ingredients:
2 **apples**, peeled, cored, and grated
2 **bananas**, mashed
14 pitted **dates**, chopped
⅓ cup blanched **almonds**, ground
¼ cup **matzah meal**
Juice and rind of ½ **lemon**
Juice and rind of ½ **orange**
¼ cup sweet **red wine**
1 teaspoon **cinnamon**
1 teaspoon **sugar**

Preparation:
Combine all ingredients, adding enough wine to make a **paste**.

Exotic Charoset

Ingredients:
1 pound **dates**
½ cup granulated **sugar**
1 teaspoon fresh **lemon juice**

Preparation:
Cover dates with warm water and **soak** overnight. **Drain** liquid into saucepan. **Chop** dates in processor, return them to pot and **cook** in liquid until soft. **Cool. Puree** dates and cooking liquid in blender and add more water, if necessary, to make it watery. **Boil** for 5 minutes and strain, squeezing out all liquid. Reserve pulp. Return liquid charoset to pot, add sugar and lemon juice. Cook on **low** heat, stirring occasionally, until reduced to thick consistency. **Add** some liquid charoset to pulp to soften and sweeten it. This makes 2 varieties of charoset - the traditional liquid and a thicker one. Serve in small bowls topped with coarsely chopped walnuts.

European Charoset

Ingredients:
1 pound (about 3) **apples**, cored and grated
½ cup **almonds** or **walnuts**, chopped
2 tablespoons **honey**
1 teaspoon ground **cinnamon**
Dash of **ginger**
About ¼ cup sweet **red wine**

Preparation:
Combine & mix to create a **thick** paste. Yields about **2** **cups.**

Rhodes Styles Charoset

Ingredients:
½ cup pitted **dates**, finely chopped
½ cup **raisins**
1 **orange**, peeled, seeded, and chopped
¼ cup **honey**
½ cup **almonds**, finely chopped
Cinnamon to taste
About ¼ cup sweet **red wine**

Preparation:
Cook dates, raisins, orange, and honey, **stirring**, until thick (about 20 minutes). Remove from heat and **add** remaining ingredients.

Moroccan Charoset

Ingredients:
1 cup **dates**, chopped
1 cup **walnuts**, chopped
Sweet **red wine**

Preparation:
Combine all ingredients, adding enough wine to create a **paste.**

Appetizers & Salads

Appetizers & Salads

Chopped Liver

Ingredients:
2 tablespoons **oil**
I pound **beef liver**
I pound **chicken liver**
2-3 medium size **onions**
3 hard boiled **eggs**

Preparation:
Wash and lightly salt liver. **Broil** until tender. Put in bowl and chop. Place onions in skillet and **sauté** in oil. **Add** sautéed onions and a little oil to bowl with liver. **Add** eggs to same bowl and **chop** slightly until eggs are absorbed in liver. **Add** a little more oil depending on desired consistency.

Grate egg and sprinkle on top of liver and **serve** on a bed of lettuce surrounded by tomatoes, green peppers, radishes, and cucumbers.

Stuffed Cabbage

Ingredients:

1½ pounds **ground beef**
1 large head **green cabbage**
1 **apple**, peeled and chopped
2 ounces **golden raisins**
1 cup **tomato puree**
1 cup whole **tomatoes**, peeled
1 medium **onion**, chopped
2 tablespoons **sugar**
2 tablespoons **apricot preserves**
1 cup **cold water**
Pinch of **white pepper**

Preparation:

Place head of cabbage in the freezer for 24 hours. **Remove** from freezer and **thaw. Peel** large leaves to be used for cabbage rolls. **Chop** the remainder of the cabbage and use it to line the bottom of a large pot.

Add tomato puree, tomatoes, water, onion, apple, raisins, sugar, and apricot preserves to the pot. **Mix** the ground beef with white pepper. **Stuff** cabbage leaves with approximately 2½ ounces of meat. **Place** carefully in pot and cover. **Bring** gravy to a **boil**.

Remove cover and **simmer** for 1¾ hours, while **stirring** occasionally. **Remove** cooked cabbage from pot with a large serving spoon.
Serves 10.

Mini Munchkin Meatballs

Ingredients:

1 pound **ground beef**
Onion and **garlic powder** to taste
1 **egg**
¼ cup **matzah meal**
12 ounces **chili sauce** or **tomato sauce**
½ cup **brown sugar**
¼ cup **lemon juice**
18 ounces **water**

Preparation:

Combine and **mix** ground beef, garlic powder, onion powder, egg, and matzah meal. **Form** into ½ inch balls and set aside. **Pour** chili or tomato sauce into medium saucepan. **Fill** the saucepan with water, **shake** well, and **add** to pot.

Add the brown sugar and lemon juice, and **mix**. **Bring** sauce to a **boil** and drop in meatballs. **Return** to boil, cover, and simmer for approximately **20 minutes.**

Sunny Salad

Ingredients:
1 can **artichoke hearts,** drained
6 tablespoons **lemon juice**
1 teaspoon **salt**
¼ teaspoon **lemon pepper**
⅓ cup **oil**
2 **avocados**, peeled and sliced
16 **cherry tomatoes** (or 2 medium tomatoes, quartered)
8 **endives**
1 small **onion**, thinly sliced
Iceberg or other **lettuce**

Preparation:
24 hours before serving, **combine** and mix lemon juice, salt, lemon pepper, oil, and mustard in glass bowl or jar until well **blended.** Add artichoke hearts and **marinate** overnight.

Just before serving, drain artichokes, reserving dressing. **Arrange** avocados, tomatoes, endives, and artichoke hearts on lettuce, with onion slices on top. When ready to serve, add reserved dressing. **Serves 8.**

Eggplant Salad

Ingredients:
3 pounds **eggplant**
1 red bell **pepper**, cored
2 medium size **onions**
6 tablespoons **olive oil**, divided
1 clove **garlic**, minced
1 teaspoon **salt**
½ teaspoon **sugar**
¼ teaspoon **oregano**
⅛ teaspoon **black pepper**
2 cups canned **plum tomatoes**, drained
2 tablespoons **lemon juice**
2 tablespoons **parsley**, chopped

Preparation:
Slice eggplant lengthwise and **cut** into ½ inch, half moon slices. **Cut** pepper in julienne strips. **Peel** onions and **slice** into thin rounds. **Place** 3 tablespoons olive oil in a large skillet. **Sauté** sliced onions and pepper strips until soft (about 5 minutes).

Add garlic and eggplant. **Cover** and **cook,** stirring occasionally, until eggplant is done (about 10 minutes). **Add** salt, sugar, oregano, and pepper. **Cook** about 2 more minutes, stirring occasionally.

Remove from heat and **stir** in tomatoes. **Transfer** to large bowl. **Mix** in remaining olive oil and lemon juice. **Chill** at least 4 hours. Serve sprinkled with parsley. **Serves 8.**

Israeli Salad with Water Chestnuts

Ingredients:

1 long **cucumber**

8-10 **plum tomatoes** or 4 **medium tomatoes**, seeded and diced

½ cup chopped **onions** (red, white, or yellow)

2 cups **water chestnuts**, chopped

½ cup **parsley**, chopped

2-4 tablespoons **olive oil**

2-3 tablespoons fresh **lemon juice**

Salt and freshly ground **black pepper** to taste

Preparation:

  Peel cucumber and **cut** into small dice. **Mix** cucumbers with tomatoes, onion, water chestnuts, and parsley. **Add** oil, lemon juice, salt, and pepper to taste. **Serve** cold or at room temperature.

  If making the salad more than a few hours ahead, **don't add** salt until ready to serve or vegetables will become watery. **Serves 8.**

Herring Salad

Ingredients:

3 fillets of **salt herring**, sliced into ½ inch pieces
1 **onion**, sliced thinly
2 **green peppers**, diced
1 cup **cabbage**, shredded
2 **tomatoes**, cubed
1 cup **lettuce**, shredded
6 **radishes**, sliced thinly
3 tablespoons **olive oil**
⅓ cup **vinegar**
¼ teaspoon freshly ground **black pepper**
2 teaspoons **sugar**

Preparation:

In a bowl, **combine** herring, onion, green peppers, cabbage, tomatoes, lettuce, and radishes. **Toss** lightly. **Mix** together olive oil, vinegar, pepper, and sugar. **Pour** over herring mixture. **Chill** for **1 hour.**

Creamy Potato Salad

Ingredients:

5 pounds **red potatoes**, with skins
2 cups **mayonnaise**
1 large **onion**, finely diced
2 stalks **celery**, finely diced
3 **carrots**, finely diced
1 **green pepper**, finely diced
6 hard boiled **eggs**, finely diced
3 tablespoons fresh **chives**, finely chopped
20 **green olives**, finely chopped
2 tablespoons **cider vinegar**
1 tablespoon **sugar**
½ teaspoon **salt**
1 teaspoon **black pepper**

Preparation:

Peel potatoes, and **boil** until just about done, approximately **20 minutes.** Let **cool**, then **slice** or **dice** potatoes. **Mix** other ingredients and **add** to potatoes while still warm. Serve chilled. **Serves 6 - 8.**

Marinated Vegetable Salad

Ingredients:
1 head **broccoli**, chopped
1 head **cauliflower**, chopped
8 ounces **mushrooms**, quartered
1 **onion**, diced
1 **green pepper**, sliced
1 **red pepper**, sliced
1 **cucumber**, sliced
1 bunch **green onions**, sliced
1 bottle zesty **Italian salad dressing**

Preparation:
Mix all vegetables. **Add** salad dressing and **marinate** at least **4 hours** or overnight. **Serves 8 - 10.**

Springtime Salad

Ingredients:
2 tart green **apples**, thinly sliced
Juice of 2 **limes**
Grated zest of 1 **lime**
2 cans **artichoke hearts**, drained and chopped
6 **scallions**, sliced
2 large **cucumbers**, peeled, seeded, thinly sliced
2 stalks **celery**, chopped
8 pitted **green olives**, sliced
1 teaspoon **horseradish**, grated
2 tablespoons **olive oil**
2 **avocados**, peeled, sliced
1 cup seedless **green grapes**
4 sprigs **parsley**
Salt to taste
Freshly ground **white pepper** to taste

Preparation:
   Place apples in a large bowl and sprinkle with lime juice. **Add** grated zest, artichoke hearts, scallions, cucumbers, celery, green olives, and horseradish. **Add** olive oil and stir to coat mixture well. **Cover** and **chill** for 1 hour. **Arrange** avocado slices and grapes over salad and sprinkle with parsley. **Serves 8.**

Soups

Soups

Traditional Chicken Soup

Ingredients:

1 large stewing **chicken**, cut in quarters
3 quarts **water** or enough to cover chicken in pot
1 large **onion**, sliced
2 large **carrots**, sliced
2 stalks **celery** with leaves, sliced
1 **parsnip**, quartered
6 sprigs **parsley**
¼ cup fresh **dill**, chopped
Salt and **pepper** to taste

Preparation:

Wash and **pat** dry chicken, and **place** in a large soup pot. **Add** water and **bring** to a boil. **Lower** heat and simmer. **Skim** fat from top which forms on surface of water. **Cover** pot and continue to **simmer** for 30 minutes.

Add onions, carrots, celery, and parsnip and continue to **simmer** slowly for about one hour. **Add** parsley, dill, salt, and pepper. **Cook** 30 minutes longer, or until chicken is tender. Allow to cool. Remove chicken and **strain** vegetables. Chill in refrigerator and remove fat that has formed on top. Makes about **2½ quarts** soup.

Chicken Beef Soup

Ingredients:

2 large **onions**
1 large **turnip**
2 **parsnips**
3 **carrots**
3 **celery** stalks
1 medium **zucchini**
1 small bunch **parsley**
1 bunch **fresh dill**
3 pounds **beef flanken**
1 (3 pound) **chicken**, cleaned and cut in quarters
2 tablespoons **salt**
1 teaspoon freshly ground **white pepper**
1 tablespoon **cumin**
1 tablespoon **curry** (optional)

Preparation:

Clean, **wash** and set aside all vegetables. With string, **tie** parsley and dill together in bundle. In large stock pot, **place** beef and chicken. **Add** cold water to cover, up to 4 quarts. **Set** on medium high heat and bring to a boil.

Skim off froth until soup is clear. **Add** all vegetables and seasonings, except parsley and dill. **Cover** pot and **reduce** heat. Simmer **2 hours. Add** parsley and dill and **cook** 15 minutes more. **Adjust** seasonings. **Serve** with matzah balls (recipe on page 34). **Serves 12.**

Beef Onion Soup

Ingredients:

4 cups **onions**, thinly sliced
3 tablespoons **margarine**
½ pound **ground beef**
2 tablespoons **matzah meal**
1 teaspoon **celery salt**
¾ teaspoon **pepper**
¾ teaspoon **garlic powder**
4 cups **beef broth** or **beef bouillon**

Preparation:

Cook onions in large saucepan over low heat in margarine for approximately **30 minutes,** stirring occasionally. **Add** soy sauce and beef. **Stir** to break up meat. **Cover** and **cook** for **15 minutes.**

Stir in matzah meal and other seasonings. **Add** beef broth and **bring** to boil. **Reduce** heat and **simmer** 5 minutes. **Serves 6.**

Fluffy Matzah Balls

Ingredients:
2 medium **eggs**
4 tablespoons **shortening**
⅛ teaspoon **salt**
Pinch of **pepper**
¾ cup **matzah meal**

Preparation:
Combine eggs, shortening, salt, and pepper. **Add** matzah meal (more if necessary to form very thick batter). **Place** in refrigerator for about 1 hour.

Half hour **before** serving, wet hands with cold water and **shape** into small balls. **Drop** into boiling water. **Don't** crowd. **Cover** tightly and **cook** for **20 minutes. Drain** and serve in chicken soup. Yields approximately **8 matzah balls.**

Traditional Homemade Borscht

Ingredients:

2 bunches **beets**
2 quarts **water**
1 **onion**, minced
2 teaspoons **salt**
2 tablespoons **sugar**
¼ cup plus 1 teaspoon **lemon juice**
2 **eggs**

Preparation:

Pare beets. **Slice** half the beets and **grate** the other half. **Bring** beets, water, onion, salt, and sugar to a boil in 4 quart saucepan. **Add** 1 teaspoon lemon juice. **Cook** for **20 minutes. Cool** and **add** remaining lemon juice.

Beat eggs and **stir** in a little borscht into eggs. **Blend** eggs with cooled borscht until well mixed. **Serve** hot or cold. Yields **1½** quarts.

Traditional Cabbage Soup

Ingredients:

1½ head **cabbage**, shredded
1 medium **onion**
Celery leaves of 2 stalks
1 tablespoon **butter** or **oil**
6 cups **soup stock**, or equivalent made from bouillon
¼ cup **sugar**
¼ cup **lemon juice**
Salt and **pepper**
Sprig of **dill**, cut

Preparation:

Heat butter or oil on low flame in a saucepan. **Add**
onion, cabbage, and celery leaves. **Saut** covered for 30 minutes and **stir** constantly until moisture has evaporated.

Add sugar and **stir** until cabbage is glazed and looks
slightly caramelized. **Add** stock. **Cover** and **simmer** 15 minutes. **Add** remaining ingredients and simmer uncovered 10
minutes.

Vegetable Soup

Ingredients:

2 tablespoons **oil**
1 large **onion**, finely chopped
2 medium **celery** stalks, finely diced
1 medium **potato**, peeled, finely diced
2 medium **carrots**, finely diced
6 cups **water**
2 **vegetable bouillon** cubes
Handful of **celery leaves**
½ teaspoon ground **cumin**
2 cups **cauliflower**, finely chopped
Salt and freshly ground **black pepper** to taste
1 cup **lettuce**, finely shredded
1 tablespoon fresh **dill**, minced
2 **scallions**, minced

Preparation:

Heat oil in large soup pot. **Add** onion and celery and **sauté** over moderate heat until golden. **Add** potato, carrots, water, bouillon cubes, celery leaves, and cumin. **Bring** to a **boil,** then **lower** heat, **cover,** and **simmer** for 15 minutes or until vegetables are nearly tender.

Add cauliflower and continue to simmer 10 minutes more. **Add** salt and pepper as desired and **remove** from heat. Let soup **cool,** then **refrigerate** overnight.

Heat soup just before serving. **Add** remaining ingredients and simmer over very low heat for **10 - 15 minutes. Add** more water if vegetables seem crowded, and adjust seasonings.

Tasty Tomato Soup

Ingredients:
¼ cup **oil**
1½ cups **onion**, chopped
¾ cup **carrots**, chopped
4 teaspoons **garlic**, minced
Salt to taste
⅛-¼ teaspoon **cayenne pepper**
4 cups **chicken broth**
4 pounds **tomatoes**, peeled, seeded, chopped, and divided
2 ripe **avocados**
2-3 teaspoons fresh **lemon juice**
¼-½ teaspoon **cumin**

Preparation:
Heat oil over medium heat. **Add** carrots and garlic and cook, **stirring** occasionally until carrots are softened (about 15 minutes). **Add** salt, cayenne pepper, and broth and sim**mer** 30 minutes. **Add** 3 pounds of the tomatoes and **cook 20 minutes.**

Pur e soup in batches and **stir** in remaining tomatoes and season. **Refrigerate** at least 8 hours. Just before serving, **peel** and **mash** avocados; **add** in lemon juice, salt, and cumin. **Stir** soup and ladle into chilled bowls. **Top** each serving with a large dollop of avocado mixture. **Serves 6.**

Chilled Cherry Soup

Ingredients:
2 cans (14 ounces each) sweet **pitted cherries**
4 cups **water**
3 whole **cloves**
1 stick **cinnamon**
¼ cup **sugar**
2 tablespoons **potato starch**
1 cup sweet **red wine**
Juice and grated rinds of 2 **lemons**

Preparation:
   Drain cherries and place in large pot. **Add** 4 cups water, cloves, cinnamon, and sugar, and **heat** over medium heat to just below boiling point. **Put** potato starch into small bowl, **add** wine, and **stir** to **dissolve. Add** lemon juice and rinds. **Remove** pot from heat and **stir** in potato starch mixture.

   Return pot to heat and cook, **stirring** constantly, until the liquid thickens. Let the soup **cool,** then **transfer** to a nonmetal container. **Serve** chilled with a dollop of sour cream. **Serves 8.**

*Q*ppetizing Asparagus Soup

Ingredients:
4½-5 cups **vegetable broth** or **chicken broth**
¼ teaspoon **saffron**
⅓ cup **pistachios** or **pine nuts**, shelled
3½ pounds **asparagus** (about 3 large bunches)
1 large russet **potato**, peeled and cubed
3 tablespoons dry white wine
¼ cup **margarine**
½ cup fresh flat leaf **parsley**, chopped
Salt and fresh ground **black pepper** to taste

Preparation:
In small saucepan, bring ½ cup broth to a **boil**. **Remove** from heat. **Add** saffron to hot broth and steep, **stirring** occasionally for 15 minutes. In dry, heavy skillet, **toast** nuts over moderate heat, **stirring** occasionally. **Remove** from heat when fragrant and slightly browned. **Chop** nuts.

Trim asparagus and cut into 2 inch pieces, set aside tips separately. **Cook** asparagus tips in boiling salted water to cover, for 2 minutes, then **transfer** to ice cold water to stop cooking. **Drain** tips well and **pat** dry.

Melt margarine in medium pot. Add asparagus stalks and cook over moderate heat, **stirring** occasionally for 3 minutes. **Stir** in potato, saffron mixture, white wine and 3 ½ cups broth, and **simmer,** covered, until vegetables are tender (approximately 20 minutes).

With an immersion blender, **blend** mixture until smooth. (Alternatively, you can **transfer** mixture to a regular blender and **blend** in batches). **Return** blended mixture to pot and **stir** in enough remaining broth to reach desired consistency. **Add** half of asparagus tips, and **bring** soup to a simmer. While soup is heating, **add** salt and pepper. **Ladle** into bowls and top each bowl with remaining asparagus tips, nuts, and parsley. **Serves 6.**

Fish

Fish

Festive Fish

Ingredients:

1 (3-4 pound) whole **fish** for baking
Salt and **pepper**
2 tablespoons fresh **lemon juice**
1 cup **onions**, chopped
½ cup **parsley**, finely chopped
3 cloves **garlic**, minced
¼ cup **oil**
1 cup **ketchup**
1 cup **tomato juice**
½ cup dry **white wine**
Lemon slices
Parsley for garnish

Preparation:

Rinse fish in cold water and **dry** thoroughly. **Sprinkle** inside and out with salt, pepper, and lemon juice. **Place** in large baking dish. In large skillet, **sauté** onions, parsley, and garlic in oil until onions are transparent. **Stir** in ketchup, tomato juice, and wine; **simmer** gently for about 3 minutes.

Pour mixture over prepared fish. **Bake,** uncovered, at **350 degrees. Baste** occasionally, allowing about 16 minutes per round. **Serve** with thin slices of lemon and sprigs of parsley. **Serves 6.**

Pickled Salmon

Ingredients:
4 cups **water**
2 **onions**, sliced
6 **salmon steaks**, about 1 inch thick
⅔ teaspoons **salt**
2 **bay leaves**
8 **black peppercorns**
1 teaspoon **brown sugar**
⅔ cup **white vinegar**

Preparation:
Bring water to a **boil** in saucepan set over high heat. **Add** onions and cook for 5 minutes. **Add** salmon steaks, bay leaves, salt, peppercorns, and brown sugar. **Cover** and **simmer** over low heat, with liquid boiling very gently, for 30 minutes.

Carefully **remove** fish and **place** in a casserole. **Stir** vinegar into the cooking liquid, then **pour** it over fish. **Chill. Serves 6.**

Poached Salmon
with Horseradish Sauce

Ingredients:

1 medium **onion**, quartered
12 whole **black peppercorns**
1 **bay leaf**
3 slices of **lemon**
4 **salmon fillets**, about ½ pound each, halved
Horseradish sauce (recipe to follow)

Preparation:

Fill a deep pan with 2 inches of water. Pan should be large enough to fit all fish in one layer. **Add** onion, peppercorns, bay leaf, and lemon, **cover** pan and **boil** for 5 minutes. **Reduce** heat to a **simmer** and gently **slide** salmon fillets into the liquid. **Cover** and **poach** very gently until fish is opaque and flakes easily when tested with a fork (about **20 minutes**).

Carefully **remove** immediately and set aside to cool. **Place** fish on chilled plates. **Top** each serving with a dollop of horseradish sauce and **serve** remaining sauce separately. **Serves 8.**

Horseradish Sauce
Ingredients:

¼ cup fresh **dill**, finely chopped
½-1 cup **mayonnaise**, to taste
¼ cup white **horseradish**, grated
Freshly ground **white pepper**
1 teaspoon fresh **lemon juice**

Preparation:

Combine all ingredients and **set aside** at room temperature for **30 minutes** to allow flavors to develop.

Yemenite Fish

Ingredients:
1 tablespoon **cumin seeds**
5-6 cloves **garlic**
2-3 tablespoons **oil**
1 cup **water**
2 tablespoons **tomato paste**
1 small **red chili pepper**, seeded
5 slices **carp** (about 3 pounds)

Preparation:
Crush cumin and garlic in oil. **Cook** oil over low to medium heat in pan large enough to hold fish and sauce. **Sauté** the cumin-garlic mixture about 1 minute, until it starts to color.

Add water, tomato paste and chili pepper. **Bring** to a **boil** and add a little water if sauce looks too dry. **Reduce** heat to **low**. **Place** fish in sauce and **simmer**, covered, for **30** minutes. Serves 8 - 10.

Traditional Gefilte Fish

Ingredients:

5 pounds assorted kosher **fish** (white fish, yellow pike, carp)
4 **eggs**
7 medium **onions**
5 **carrots**
1 teaspoon **sugar**
3 tablespoons **salt**
1-4 tablespoons **matzah meal**
1½ cups **water**
1 teaspoon **pepper**

Preparation:

Fillet fish and reserve skin, heads and bones. **Grind** fish fillets, together with 2 onions and 1 carrot in food grinder. **Place** mixture in wooden chopping bowl. **Add** eggs, one at a time, while **chopping** well with wooden chopper, so eggs are thoroughly blended into mixture. **Add** 1 tablespoon salt, pepper, and sugar and **alternate** adding matzah meal with water. Keep **chopping** between additions. **Chop** until soft and light and mixture sticks to chopper. Let **stand** for 10 minutes.

Slice remaining carrots and onions and **place** into a large pot, together with reserved skin, heads and bones and remaining salt and pepper. **Cover** with water and **bring** to a **boil. Wet** hands with cold water, **take** heaping tablespoons of chopped fish and **form** into oval or round patties. Carefully, **add** fish patties to cooking broth. **Add** more boiling water, if needed to cover fish. **Cover** pot. **Bring** rapidly to **boil,** then **simmer** for about 2 hours until broth is reduced to about ¼ of the original volume.

Allow to **cool** about 1 hour before removing fish and carrots from pot. **Strain** liquid. **Serve** fish hot or cold with some of the liquid. **Garnish** with sliced carrots.

Spinach Stuffed Fillets

Ingredients:
I pound **spinach**
I **onion**, chopped
I tablespoon **butter** or **margarine**
Salt and **pepper** to taste
I ½ pounds **fish fillets**
I **egg**, beaten
¼ cup **matzah meal**

Preparation:
  Wash spinach thoroughly. **Cook** spinach and onion together using only the water that clings to the leaves. When tender, **drain** and **chop. Add** butter and seasonings to taste. Let **cool. Cut** fillets in 2 inch strips. **Add** egg and matzah meal to cooled spinach. **Spread** mixture on each fillet. **Roll** and **secure** with toothpick. Set oven to **400 degrees**, and **cook** for **20 minutes**.

Red Snapper

Ingredients:

½ cup **red onion**, minced
4 pounds small **red snappers**
Salt to taste
1 teaspoon **sugar**
¼ cup **red wine vinegar**
½ cup **olive oil**
1 cup dark **seedless raisins**
½ cup **pine nuts**

Preparation:

Preheat **oven** to **400 degrees.** Lightly oil 13x9 inch baking pan and **scatter** onion into pan. **Sprinkle** fish lightly with salt and **place** on top of onion. **Dissolve** sugar in vinegar and **pour** over fish. **Pour** oil over fish. **Scatter** raisins and pine nuts over the top.

Cover and **bake** about 15 minutes. **Reduce** heat to **375 degrees, baste** fish and **bake** uncovered **20 - 30 minutes** longer, until liquid is almost entirely evaporated and fish is golden. **Serves 12.**

Whitefish with Dill Sauce

Ingredients:
4 (6 ounce) **whitefish fillets**
½ cup **mayonnaise**
1 teaspoon melted **butter** or **margarine**
1 bunch **fresh dill**, finely chopped

Preparation:
Preheat **oven** to **400 degrees. Combine** mayonnaise, butter or margarine, and dill in small bowl and **mix** well. **Place** fish in greased baking dish and **pour** dill mixture on top.

Bake in oven for **7 - 8 minutes. Serves 4.**

Dairy
Delights

Dairy Delights

Matzah Lasagna

Ingredients:

3 matzahs
2 eggs
1 can **tomato mushroom sauce**
8 ounces **cottage cheese**
8 slices **American cheese**
Salt and **pepper** to taste

Preparation:

Place matzahs in bowl and **cover** with boiling water. **Drain** immediately. **Beat** eggs, salt, and pepper, **pour** over matzahs.

In large casserole dish, **alternate** layers of tomato-mushroom sauce, matzah, cottage cheese, and American cheese in order. **Bake** at 350 degrees for 20 minutes.

Cheese Blintzes

Batter
Ingredients:
⅔ cup **cake meal**
½ teaspoon **salt**
1½ cups **water**
3 **eggs**

Preparation:
Combine cake meal and salt. In separate bowl, **combine** eggs and water. Gradually **add** egg mixture to cake meal, **beating** well to prevent lumps. Allow air bubbles to settle before starting to fry batter.

Pour (in circular motion to form pancake) 3 tablespoons batter into lightly greased frying pan. **Fry** until batter sets and curls at edges. **Turn out** onto cloth.

Cheese Filling
Ingredients:
1 pound **farmer cheese**
1 **egg**
½ teaspoon **salt**
¼ cup **sugar**
¼ teaspoon **cinnamon**

Preparation:
Mash cheese and combine with other ingredients. Place 3 heaping tablespoons on center of each pancake. **Fold** in side edges and roll.

Fry in small quantity of oil or butter until browned on both sides.

Crustless Quiche

Ingredients:

1 eggplant (about 1½ pounds)
1 tablespoon coarse kosher salt
4 medium tomatoes (about 1½ pounds)
1 large onion, chopped coarsely
¼ cup parsley, finely chopped
1 teaspoon dried thyme
1 teaspoon dried basil
10 ounces mozzarella cheese
1¼ cups matzah meal
1½ cups milk
1 cup cottage cheese
Salt and freshly ground white pepper to taste
Few grains nutmeg, freshly grated

Preparation:

Cut unpeeled eggplant into slices ½ inch thick. Sprinkle both sides with salt. Drain for ½ hour on paper towels. Cut tomatoes into slices ½ inch thick. Set aside.

Combine onion, parsley, thyme, and basil in small dish and sprinkle lightly with salt. Set aside. Coarsely shred mozzarella and set aside (should be about 2½ cups).

Lightly butter or oil a 13x9x2½ inch baking dish. Preheat oven to 350 degrees. Rinse eggplant slices well. Pat dry with paper towel. In a large frying pan, heat about ¾ cup of oil until hot but not smoking. Dust eggplant slices with matzah meal. Turning carefully with tongs, sauté slices until golden brown on both sides. This is usually done in 2 batches. Add remaining oil as needed. Drain eggplant on paper towels.

Using tongs, carefully transfer eggplant to prepared baking dish. If necessary, cut slices so eggplant fits evenly. Layer tomato slices over eggplant. Sprinkle with onion mixture. Cover with mozzarella. Place milk, eggs, and cottage cheese in blender and process until smooth and mixture begins to look like custard. Season with salt, pepper, and nutmeg. Pour custard mixture over vegetables.

Bake about 40 minutes or until dish is light golden brown and the custard is set. Serve warm or as a cold entrée. Serves 8 - 10.

Fabulous French Toast

Ingredients:

½ cup **milk**
2 **eggs**, well beaten
1 tablespoon grated **lemon** or **orange rind**
6-8 slices **sponge cake** (about 1 inch thick)
Unsalted **butter** or **margarine**
Cinnamon and **sugar** to taste

Preparation:

In a large shallow bowl, **combine** milk, eggs, and lemon/orange peel and **mix** well. **Soak** sponge cake slices in milk mixture.

Melt butter in frying pan. **Fry** cake on both sides until brown. **Sprinkle** with cinnamon and sugar, if desired. **Serves 4.**

ℳatzah Pizza

Ingredients:
Matzah
Olive Oil
Tomato Sauce
Grated **Mozzarella Cheese**
Oregano

Preparation:
Preheat **oven** to **450 degrees**. **Place** matzah on lightly greased baking sheet. **Spread** a very thin layer of olive oil over matzah, then **add** sauce, cheese, oregano, and other desired toppings.
Bake for **10 - 15 minutes,** watching carefully to keep from burning.

Bubby's Famous Matzah Brei

Ingredients:
4 matzahs
4 large eggs
2 tablespoons oil
Pinch of salt
Dash of pepper

Preparation:

Run each matzah under hot water for 5 - 10 seconds. Set aside to soften for 1 - 2 minutes. Beat eggs, salt, and pepper together in large bowl. Break matzah into small pieces (2 - 3 inch squares) and stir into egg mixture.

Add oil to skillet and heat over medium flame. Add matzah/egg mixture and brown on one side. Flip and brown on other side. Serves 3 - 4.

Variations:

Add a bit of cinnamon and sugar to the beaten eggs. Serve with honey, applesauce, or jelly.

For a spicy version, add ¼ cup grated onion, additional pepper, and/or chopped scallions. Serve with sour cream.

To sweeten, add raisins or honey to beaten eggs. and sprinkle sugar on top of finished matzah brei.

Swiss Apple Pancakes

Ingredients:

3 matzahs
6 eggs, well beaten
2 apples, peeled and grated
2 tablespoons sugar
½ teaspoon salt
Matzah meal
Oil for frying

Preparation:

Place matzahs in pan with enough water to cover. Soak matzahs in water until soft, then drain. Combine eggs with apples, sugar, and salt and mix well. Add egg mixture to moistened matzahs and blend thoroughly. Add about ½ cup of matzah meal or enough for frying consistency and drop by spoonfuls into frying pan coated with ½ inch vegetable oil. Fry until golden brown. Serve with powdered sugar, stewed fruit, and/or maple syrup.

Spinach, Potato, Cheese Souffle

Ingredients:

3 medium **potatoes**
2 (10 ounce) packages frozen chopped **spinach**, thawed and drained
3 green **onions**, chopped
8 ounces **ricotta cheese**
Juice of ½ **lemon**
Pinch of **salt** and **pepper** to taste
1 cup shredded **mozzarella cheese**
4 **matzahs**

Preparation:

Preheat oven to **400 degrees. Place** potatoes in oven, and **bake 45 minutes,** or until tender. Let cool, **peel** and **cut** into ¼ inch slices.

Reduce oven to **350 degrees.** In medium bowl, **stir** spinach, green onions, ricotta cheese, lemon juice, salt, and pepper.

Wet matzahs under **warm** water briefly on each side, until flexible. **Place** one in bottom of 9 inch square baking dish. Spread ¼ of the ricotta/spinach mixture over it, followed by a layer of potato slices. **Sprinkle** ¼ of the mozzarella cheese over potatoes. **Repeat** layers, and finish with mozzarella cheese on top.

Bake for **35 minutes** in preheated oven, or until cheese on top is golden brown. **Serve** warm. **Cut** into squares.

Meat & Poultry

Meat & Poultry

Chickens in Apricot Sauce

Ingredients:

2 rock cornish **chickens**
1 small **onion**, diced very fine
1 jar **apricot jam**
½ cup **ketchup**

Preparation:

Combine diced onion, jam, and ketchup and **rub** over chickens.
Place chickens in roasting pan, **cover** and **bake** at **325 degrees** for
45 minutes.

Uncover and continue to **bake** at **350 degrees** for additional
15 - 30 minutes to brown. **Baste** often.

Chicken Sauté with Potatoes

Ingredients:
4-5 pounds **chicken pieces**
Lemon
Coarse **Kosher salt**
Freshly ground **black pepper** to taste
5 tablespoons **peanut oil**
5 medium **potatoes**, peeled, cut into 2-inch cubes
¼ cup **parsley**, snipped or chopped
¾ teaspoon dried **chervil**
¼ teaspoon dried **tarragon**
Pinch of dried **thyme**
¾ cup dry **white wine**
Additional **salt** to taste

Preparation:
Rub chicken pieces with cut lemon. **Sprinkle** with salt and pepper.
Heat oil until hot, but not smoking, in a large pan or heavy skillet with a
tight fitting lid. **Sauté** chicken pieces, skin side down, for **5 - 6 minutes.**
Turn chicken and **sauté** for **another** 5 - 6 minutes, **adding** more oil if
necessary. Remove chicken to large platter.

In same pan, **sauté** potatoes for **3 - 4 minutes. Shake** several times to
prevent sticking. **Remove** potatoes to another plate. **Return** chicken to
skillet. **Cover** chicken with potatoes, and **sprinkle** with herbs. **Add** wine
and about ½ teaspoon of salt. **Cover** tightly. **Simmer** for **25 - 30
minutes. Pierce** chicken with fork to test if done. Juices should run clear,
with no hint of pink color. **Serves 6 - 8.**

Festive Roast Chicken

Ingredients:

2 (2 pound) **broilers**
3-4 whole **pears**, peeled and pared
½ cup **dry wine**
1 cup **orange juice**

Preparation:

Quarter broilers and **marinate** in wine for 1 hour. Arrange chickens in greased pan with pears. **Baste** occasionally with orange juice. Roast 1½ hours at 325 degrees.

Chicken a la King

Ingredients:

4 tablespoons **shortening**
1 cup **mushrooms**, sliced
1 small **onion**, chopped
4 tablespoons **potato starch**, mixed into cold water
2 cups **chicken soup** (or 1 can of chicken soup mixed with enough to cold water to make 2 cups)
2 cups cooked **chicken** or **turkey**, cut into small pieces
Dash of **pepper**
Dash of **paprika**

Preparation:

Sauté onion and mushrooms in shortening for about 5 minutes. **Add** paprika and pepper. **Add** soup and potato starch **slowly** over low heat. This will thicken in about **3 minutes. Add** chicken and **cook** for 5-10 minutes or until warm.

Mouth Watering Meatballs

Ingredients:
2 pounds **ground beef** or mixed **ground lamb**, **veal**, and **beef**
1 large **onion**, grated
3 tablespoons **ketchup** or soft **tomato**, finely chopped
2 **carrots**, grated
1 **apple**, grated
2 **eggs**
2 teaspoons **salt**
½ teaspoon **pepper**

Preparation:
Mix all ingredients well. **Form** into balls and **cook** in simmering sauce for **1 hour**.

Sauce
Ingredients:
3 cups **water**
½ teaspoon **salt**
½ teaspoon **pepper**
1 green **pepper**, diced
2 large **onions**, diced
2 stalks **celery**
1 **tomato**
2 cloves **garlic**, minced

Preparation:
Combine all ingredients in heavy saucepan. **Bring** to a **boil**.
Variation:
To make **sweet and sour** meatballs, **add** juice of 1 lemon, or a pinch of sour salt, **and** 2 tablespoons sugar.

Brisket of Beef

Ingredients:

5 pounds **brisket** or **rolled roast**
1½ pounds **dried fruit**, mixed
¼ cup **honey** (use ½ cup if sweeter taste is desired)
2 **onions**, chopped in food processor
½ teaspoon **cinnamon**
1 tablespoon **lemon juice**
1 tablespoon **orange juice**
Salt and **pepper** to taste
2 tablespoons **vegetable oil**
3 **sweet potatoes**, peeled and sliced
6 **carrots**
1½ cups dry **red wine**

Preparation:

Preheat oven to **325 degrees**. **Heat** oil in 5 quart casserole. **Brown** meat on all sides. **Remove** meat and **add** onions. **Cook** onions until slightly browned. **Return** meat; **add** wine, salt, and pepper. **Bring** to a **boil** and **cover**. **Bake** for **1 hour**.

Add dried fruit, sweet potatoes, carrots, lemon juice, honey, orange juice, and cinnamon to the meat. **Replace** cover and **cook 2½ - 3½ hours** until meat is tender. **Add** more wine if necessary during cooking for extra flavor. **Garnish** with orange slices and parsley. **Serves 8.**

Sweet and Sour Pot Roast

Ingredients:

2½ pound **pot roast**, cut in large chunks
Vegetable oil
1 cup **onion**, sliced
2 cloves **garlic**, peeled and minced
¾ cup **hot water**
1 **bay leaf**
2 tablespoons **Passover red wine vinegar**
1 tablespoon **brown sugar**
3 tablespoons **ketchup**
½ cup **raisins**
1 pound **prunes**
¾ teaspoon **salt**
¼ teaspoon **pepper**
6 large **sweet potatoes**, peeled and quartered
12 small **white potatoes**, peeled

Preparation:

Sear meat on all sides in vegetable oil, adding oil as needed to keep from sticking. **Add** onions and **cook** until golden. **Add** garlic, hot water, bay leaf, vinegar, brown sugar, ketchup, raisins, prunes, salt, pepper, white and sweet potatoes. **Simmer** on low flame about **2 - 3 hours** or until tender. **Serves 6.**

Turkey with Spice

Ingredients:

1 lemon
½ navel orange
1 medium sized turkey
Grated zest of 1 whole lemon
Grated zest of 1 whole navel orange
3 tablespoons fresh ginger, grated
3 tablespoons oil
2 tablespoons fresh lemon juice
⅓ cup fresh orange juice
1 tablespoon light brown sugar
2 cloves garlic
Freshly ground pepper

Preparation:

Preheat oven to 425 degrees. Cut the lemon in half and rub the skin and inside of turkey with the cut side of one half. Discard lemon half. Place second lemon half in the turkey, together with orange half. Add garlic. Place turkey on rack and roast uncovered for 30 minutes. Lower temperature to 325 degrees.

In bowl, combine lemon and orange zest, grated ginger, oil, lemon juice, orange juice, and brown sugar to form a basting sauce. Stir basting sauce and brush over turkey. Cover turkey with sheet of aluminum foil and continue to roast for 2 hours, basting 3 more times.

Uncover turkey, baste again and continue to roast until an instant meat thermometer inserted in the thickest part of the thigh registers 180 degrees. Continue to baste the turkey until all sauce has been used. Transfer to carving plate and serve warm. Serves 8.

Cholent

Ingredients:

5 pounds **red potatoes**, peeled and grated
5 **onions**, grated
2-3 pounds **cubed meat**
3 pounds **small potatoes**
1 tablespoon **paprika**
2-3 cloves fresh **garlic**
Salt and **pepper** to taste
Water

Preparation:

Combine grated potatoes and onions. **Add** salt, pepper, paprika, and garlic. **Mix** meat into potato mixture. **Add** small potatoes with meat. **Cook** overnight on a **low** flame, adding water if necessary.

Hot Dogs in Blankets

Ingredients:
½ cup **oil**
1½ cups **water**
2 cups **matzah meal**
4 **eggs**
5 **hot dogs**, halved
1 tablespoon **sugar**
1 teaspoon **salt**

Preparation:
Combine oil and water in saucepan and bring to a **boil**. **Add** matzah meal, sugar, and salt, then **mix** thoroughly. **Remove** from heat and continue to **mix** until fully combined.

Add eggs one at a time, while mixing. **Divide** dough into 10 parts and **shape** each around each part. **Bake** in 325 degree oven on greased cookie sheet for about **20 - 30** minutes.

Veal Brisket

Ingredients:
2½-3 pounds **veal brisket**
1 can **cranberry sauce**
1 envelope (2 ounces) **onion soup mix**

Preparation:
Combine cranberry sauce and onion soup mix. **Place** veal in roasting pan. **Pour** cranberry/onion mixture over veal. **Cover** roasting pan with aluminum foil and **bake** in **350 degree** oven for **1½ - 2 hours.**

Sweet, Tasty, and Tangy Duck

Ingredients:

1 (5-6 pound) **duckling**, cut into serving pieces
½ cup plus 2 tablespoons sweet **red wine**
1 tablespoon grated **orange peel**
1 clove **garlic**, minced
3 tablespoons **peanut oil**
1 tablespoon **potato starch**
1¼ cups fresh **orange juice**
1 tablespoon **honey**
¼ teaspoon ground **ginger**
⅛ teaspoon **pepper**
1 cup fresh **orange sections**

Preparation:

Puncture duckling skin generously with fork, **place** on rack in roasting pan. **Pour** ½ cup wine over duckling pieces. **Roast** at **325 degrees, basting** occasionally, allowing about 25 minutes per pound.

In medium saucepan, lightly **sauté** orange peel and garlic in oil. **Add** potato starch, **stirring** until smooth. Slowly **add** orange juice, 2 tablespoons wine and honey; **simmer** 1 minute. **Stir** in ginger, pepper, and orange sections, **simmer** 5 minutes longer. **Serve** sauce hot with roast duckling.
Serves 4 - 6.

Kugels & Side Dishes

Kugels & Side Dishes

Passover "Bagels"

Ingredients:
½ cup oil
1 cup boiling water
2 cups matzah meal
1 tablespoon sugar
4 eggs
1 teaspoon salt

Preparation:
Bring oil and water to a boil in saucepan. Add dry ingredients all at once and beat rapidly over low heat, until mixture leaves sides of pan and forms a ball. Remove from heat and beat in eggs one at a time. Beat well after adding each egg until batter is thick and smooth.

Shape batter into about 12 bagels. Bake on well greased baking sheet at 375 degrees for 1 hour or until golden brown.

Garlic "Bread"

Ingredients:
½ cup plus 2 tablespoons **oil**
1 cup **water**
1 cup **matzah meal**
1 teaspoon **salt**
1 teaspoon fresh **basil**, chopped
4 large **eggs**
2 cloves **garlic**

Preparation:
Combine ½ cup oil and 1 cup water in saucepan, **bring** to a **boil. Remove** pan from heat and **add** matzah meal, salt, and basil together. **Stir** well with wooden spoon. **Preheat** oven to **375 degrees.**

Finely **chop** garlic. **Mix** eggs and half of garlic into matzah meal mixture with electric mixer until mixture begins to **form** a ball. **Shape** into oval loaf. **Place** on ungreased baking sheet and **bake** 40 - 50 minutes, until top is golden brown. Remove from sheet and let **cool** 10 minutes on rack.

Split in half lengthwise. **Mince** remaining garlic clove and **mix** with 2 tablespoons oil; **spread** over each half. **Toast** under broiler. **Cut** into 12 slices and **serve** immediately.

Variation:
For herb bread, **add** 2 ½ tablespoons of mixed herbs (oregano, rosemary, thyme, chives). **Decrease** garlic to 1 clove. **Mix** 2 tablespoons of mixture into dough. Instead of spreading garlic on bread before toasting, **sprinkle** with remaining herbs.

Mini Potato Knishes

Ingredients:

3 cups **mashed potatoes** (approximately 2 large russet potatoes)
2 **eggs**, slightly beaten
2 tablespoons **margarine**
1 teaspoon **salt**
⅛ teaspoon **black pepper**
⅜ cup **matzah meal**
1 **onion**, diced
1 **egg yolk** beaten with 1 tablespoon **water**
oil for baking sheet

Preparation:

Preheat oven to **400 degrees.** In medium sized bowl, **combine** mashed potatoes with eggs, margarine, salt, pepper, and matzah meal. **Sauté** diced onion until brown and **add** to mixture as well. **Form** into walnut sized balls. **Brush** with diluted egg yolk.

Place on a well greased baking sheet and bake for **20 minutes** or until well browned. Yields approximately **42** miniature knishes.

Broccoli Walnut Ring

Ingredients:
1 package (10 ounces) frozen **broccoli**, chopped
1 clove **garlic** (optional)
2 tablespoons **onion**, minced
¼ cup **margarine**, softened
1½ tablespoons **potato starch**
1 cup **water** or **bouillon**
3 **eggs**, separated
½ cup **walnuts**, chopped

Preparation:
Preheat oven to **350 degrees. Grease** a 1½ quart oven
proof ring mold with the softened margarine. **Refrigerate**
while preparing the filling. **Cook** broccoli according to
package directions, but **add** garlic clove to the water. **Drain**
well and **discard** garlic. In 1 quart saucepan over medium
heat, **sauté** the onion until soft and golden. In measuring
cup, **dissolve** the potato starch in the water or bouillon; **add**
to onions. **Cook** over low heat, **stirring** until thick and
smooth. **Cool** slightly. In mixing bowl, **beat** egg yolks until
light. **Stir** yolks, broccoli, and walnuts into onion mixture.

In separate bowl, **beat** the egg whites until **stiff. Fold**
into broccoli mixture. **Spoon** mixture into prepared ring
mold. **Set** the mold into a hot water bath that reaches
halfway up the sides of the mold. **Bake** in **preheated** oven
for **30 - 35 minutes,** until firm. Let **rest** for 5 minutes
before removing from mold. **Serves 4.**

Squash Pudding

Ingredients:
4 pounds **yellow squash**, sliced
3 medium **onions**, peeled and cut into wedges
¼ cup **boiling water**
¼ cup **butter** or **margarine**
¼ teaspoon **thyme**
⅛ teaspoon **rosemary**
⅛ teaspoon **nutmeg**
1 teaspoon **salt**
⅛ teaspoon **pepper**
1 tablespoon **brown sugar**
¼ cup **parsley**, minced

Preparation:
Preheat oven to **350 degrees. Place** squash, onions, water, and butter or margarine in large pot, covered, and **simmer** for **25 - 30 minutes. Uncover** and **simmer** 10 minutes longer, **crushing** large pieces with a fork. **Stir** in remaining ingredients.

Transfer to a greased 3 quart dish and bake, **uncovered,** in preheated oven for **2 - 2½ hours. Serves 6.**

Stuffed Mushrooms

Ingredients:

1 teaspoon **olive oil**

6 large **mushroom caps**

¼ cup **spinach**

¼ cup **mushroom stems**, cooked and chopped

2 tablespoons **green onions**, minced

1 clove **garlic**, chopped

1 **egg**

Salt and pepper

⅓ cup **matzah meal**

Preparation:

Brush olive oil on mushroom caps . **Mince** stems and **combine** with remaining ingredients **except** for matzah meal.

Fill mushroom caps with spinach mixture. **Top** with matzah meal. Bake at **350 degrees** for **15 minutes** or until mushrooms are tender and top is golden brown. **Serves 6.**

Colorful Peppers

Ingredients:

2 medium size **red peppers**
2 medium size **green peppers**
2 medium size **yellow peppers**
3 tablespoons **vegetable oil**
Kosher salt to taste, if desired
Freshly ground **black pepper** to taste

Preparation:

Rinse peppers and dry. **Cut** off tops and bottoms. **Cut** in half, **seed** and **slice** into thin strips. **Heat** saucepan until very hot. **Add** oil and heat. **Add** peppers and **stir** rapidly over **high** heat until slightly wilted. **Season** with salt and pepper. **Remove** to serving platter. **Serves 6.**

Zucchini Pudding

Ingredients:

1¾-2 pounds **zucchini**
2-3 stalks **celery**
2 **potatoes**
2-3 **carrots**
2 **onions**
1 stick **margarine**, melted
4 cubes of **bouillon**
3 cups **matzah farfel**
5 **eggs**, beaten

Preparation:

Preheat oven to **350 degrees. Grate** first 5 ingredients, then **add** rest of ingredients and **mix** well together. Bake **1½ hours** in oven or until golden brown.

Apple Fritters

Ingredients:
1 cup **matzah meal**
3 **eggs**, beaten
2 tablespoons **oil**
½ teaspoon **salt**
½ cup **water**
3 tart **apples**, thinly sliced

Preparation:
  Mix ingredients. **Fry** as pancakes. **Drain,** then **sprinkle** with sugar and cinnamon.

Delicious Asparagus

Ingredients:
1 pound **asparagus**
Water
2 tablespoons **butter** or **margarine**
¼ teaspoon **salt**
Dash of **white pepper**

Preparation:
   Wash asparagus and **trim** tough ends by snapping them.
Place in wide shallow saucepan and **cover** with cold water
by ½ inch. **Place** on high heat and **bring** to boil. **Lower**
heat to medium and **simmer** 5 - 6 minutes until asparagus
is bright green and tender. **Drain** thoroughly and **return** to
pan. **Add** butter or margarine. **Heat** over low heat until butter melts and coats asparagus. **Serves 4.**

Matzah Stuffing

Ingredients:

¾ cup **vegetable shortening**
¾ cup **onion**, minced
⅔ cup **celery**, diced
⅓ cup **pepper**, chopped
1 can **mushrooms**, (stems and pieces)
1 teaspoon **salt**
¼ teaspoon **pepper**
1 tablespoon **paprika**
3 **eggs**
2 cans clear **chicken soup**
½ cup **walnuts** (optional)
Matzahs

Preparation:

Sauté onion, celery, and green pepper in shortening until tender but not browned. **Add** broken matzahs and **toast** lightly. **Combine** seasonings, eggs, and soup. **Bake** in **350 degree** oven for **35 minutes.**

Pareve "Noodle" Kugel

Ingredients:

12 ounces wide **Passover noodles**
¾ cup **sugar**
¾ cup **raisins**
¾ **nuts**, chopped
1 teaspoon **salt**
4 **eggs**, well beaten
½ cup **butter** or **margarine**
¼ teaspoon **cinnamon**

Preparation:

Cook wide noodles according to directions on package. **Drain** well. **Add** sugar, raisins, nuts, salt, and eggs. **Melt** butter or margarine in 8x12 inch baking pan. **Grease** pan and **pour** remaining butter or margarine into noodle mixture. **Blend** well and **spread** mixture in baking pan. **Sprinkle** evenly with cinnamon. Bake in **375 degree** oven for **50 minutes** or until browned.

Potato Kugel

Ingredients:

1 small **onion**
8 **potatoes**, peeled
5 **eggs**
¼-½ cup **oil**
1 tablespoon **salt**
½-1 teaspoon **black pepper**

Preparation:

Preheat **oven** to 450 degrees. **Place** oil in 9x13 inch pan in hot oven. In large bowl, lightly **beat** eggs. **Chop** onion in food processor then **place** in bowl with beaten eggs. **Grate** potatoes in processor then **add** to bowl. **Add** salt and pepper to bowl. **Pour** boiling oil from pan into mixture.

Mix together and **place** in greased pan. **Bake** at 450 degrees for 1 hour or until top is brown.

Kishka

Ingredients:
2 stalks celery
1 small onion
¾ cup oil
1 teaspoon paprika
2 carrots
1½ teaspoon salt
1½ cups matzah meal

Preparation:
Put oil in food processor. Add salt and paprika. Cut up carrots, celery, onion, and add to oil. Process until mixture is smooth. Pour into bowl and add matzah meal. Place on foil and form into loaf. Roll foil and twist edges like a candy wrapper. Place in pan and bake in 350 degree oven for 1 hour.

Carrot Tzimmes

Ingredients:
4 cups **carrots**, diagonally sliced
1½ cups **apple juice**
½ teaspoon **salt**
⅓ cup **honey**
3 tablespoons **oil**
1 **lemon**, halved, washed and juiced
½ cup **prunes**, sliced or **raisins** (optional)

Preparation:
   Combine carrots, juice, prunes if desired, and salt in saucepan.
Bring to a boil; **boil** for 10 minutes. **Add** honey, oil, lemon juice,
and lemon halves. **Simmer** over medium flame for **30 minutes,** or
until most of the liquid is absorbed and carrots are glazed.
Garnish with additional grated lemon peel.

Honey Sweetened Potatoes

Ingredients:
8 medium **sweet potatoes** (4 pounds)
½ cup **honey**
2 tablespoons grated **orange rind**
½ cup **orange juice**
¼ cup **margarine**
½ teaspoon **cinnamon**
Dash of **ginger**
¼ teaspoon **salt**

Preparation:
Cook unpeeled sweet potatoes until tender. **Peel** and **cut** into ½ inch slices. **Combine** honey, orange rind, orange juice, margarine, cinnamon, ginger, and salt in a large skillet. Bring to a **boil,** reduce heat, and **simmer** 5 minutes. **Add** potatoes and **simmer** 5 more minutes, **basting** frequently with sauce. **Serves 8.**

Desserts

Desserts

Strawberry Shortcake

Ingredients:
Sponge Cake (recipe found on page 103)
Strawberry preserves
1 cup **heavy cream**
1 tablespoon **sugar**
Fresh **strawberries**

Preparation:
   Slice sponge cake in half horizontally using sharp knife.
Spread bottom section with strawberry preserves. **Replace** top
section. **Whip** cream and sweeten with sugar. **Frost** top of cake
with whipped cream. **Decorate** with fresh strawberries.

Chocolate Almond Cake

Ingredients:

7 **eggs**
1 cup **sugar**
1 cup **brewed coffee**
4 ounces unsweetened **chocolate**
½ pound blanched **almonds**, ground

Preparation:

Line 9 inch springform pan with wax paper or aluminum foil. Using 2 large bowls, **separate** egg yolks from egg whites. **Beat** yolks until light and lemony in color, gradually **beating** in sugar (about 20 minutes).

Meanwhile, **place** coffee and chocolate in small heavy saucepan and **heat** carefully until **blended. Add** ground almonds to yolk mixture and **blend** in melted chocolate and coffee.

Beat egg whites until they form soft peaks. **Fold** whites into batter, using a cut-and-fold motion with rubber spatula.

Transfer batter to prepared cake pan and bake in a **preheated 350 degree** oven for **45 minutes,** or until cake starts to pull away from sides of pan. Let cake cool in pan on rack. **Remove** cake from pan and invert on rack. **Remove** wax paper or aluminum foil. **Place** on cake plate or wrap cooled cake loosely in foil for storage.

Cranberry Apple Crisp

Ingredients:

2 cups **cranberries**

3 cups **apples**, peeled and coarsely chopped

1 cup **sugar**

½ teaspoon **salt**

2 cups **matzah farfel**

¾ cup **brown** or **white sugar**

½ cup **butter** or **margarine**

Preparation:

Wash cranberries, **combine** with apples and sugar and **turn** into greased 8x8 inch baking dish. **Moisten** farfel with water, **drain** immediately. **Crumble** farfel together with remaining ingredients. **Spread** over fruit. **Bake** about **50 minutes** in **350 degree** oven. **Serve** warm.

Chocolate Carrot Cake

Ingredients:
3½ ounces semisweet **chocolate**, melted and cooled
1½ cups **nuts, walnuts,** or **almonds**, ground
1 cup **carrots**, grated
4 large **eggs**, separated
Pinch of **salt**
¾ cup **sugar**
⅓ cup **matzah meal**
Rind of 1 **orange**, grated
Chocolate icing

Preparation:
Line a 9 inch springform pan with wax paper. **Grease** wax paper. **Dust** with some matzah meal. **Beat** yolks with ½ cup sugar until lemon colored. **Add** melted chocolate, beating until fully mixed in. **Stir** in matzah meal, carrots, nuts, and rind and mix well. **Beat** egg whites with salt to form soft peaks. Then **add** remaining ¼ cup sugar beating on high until sugar is fully mixed in. **Fold** gently into carrot mixture. **Bake** at **350 degrees** for **1 hour.**

Chocolate Icing
Ingredients:
6 ounces semisweet **chocolate**, melted
3 tablespoons **margarine**, softened
1 **egg** plus 1 **yolk**

Preparation:
Beat ingredients together and **pour** on cake. **Spread** to smooth. **Keep** at room temperature.

Scrumptious Nut Cake

Ingredients:
¾ cup **matzah meal**
¾ cup **potato starch**
½ teaspoon **salt**
6 egg **yolks**
1¾ cups **sugar**
1 cup **orange juice**, freshly squeezed
1½ cups **walnuts**, chopped
1 tablespoon grated **orange rind**
6 **egg whites**, stiffly beaten

Preparation:
   Mix matzah meal, potato starch, and salt. **Set aside. Beat** egg yolks until **thick.** Gradually add sugar, beating until lemon colored. **Add** matzah meal mixture, **alternating** with the orange juice. **Fold** in walnuts and orange rind. **Beat** egg whites until stiff and **fold** in. **Pour** into greased 9 inch tube pan. Bake in **325 degree** oven for **1 hour** or until lightly browned and cake shrinks away from sides of the pan. **Cool** on rack. **Serves 10 - 12.**

Chocolate Mousse Torte

Ingredients:

8 ounces **semisweet chocolate**
1 tablespoon **instant coffee** (dissolved in ¼ cup boiling water)
¼ cup **boiling water**
8 **eggs**, separated
⅔ cup **sugar**
⅛ teaspoon **salt**
Fine dry **matzah crumbs**

Preparation:

Preheat oven to **350 degrees. Place** the chocolate in the top of a double boiler over hot (not boiling) water. **Add** coffee to chocolate. **Cover** and let **cook** over very low heat. **Stir** with wire whisk occasionally.

When chocolate is almost melted, **remove** top of double boiler and **whisk** mixture until smooth.

Meanwhile, **beat** egg yolks until thick. Slowly **beat** in sugar until mixture is thick and lemon colored. **Beat** chocolate into yolk mixture. **Beat** egg whites and salt until **stiff** but not dry. **Stir** ¼ of the whites into chocolate mixture. **Fold** in remaining whites gently until blended. Set aside ⅓ of mousse mixture for the crust. Cover and refrigerate remaining ⅔ of mousse.

Coat a 9 inch pie plate with shortening. Dust with matzah crumbs. Pour reserved ⅓ of mousse mixture into prepared pan and **bake** for **25 minutes.** Turn off oven but leave cooked mousse in oven 5 minutes longer. **Remove** and **cool** for **2 hours** on a wire rack. As it cools the cooked mousse sinks in middle to form the pie shell. When the shell has cooled, **fill** with the chilled uncooked mousse, **mounding** it up like a pie filling. **Chill 2 - 3 hours.** Serves 8.

Seven Layer Cake

Ingredients:

3½ ounces bittersweet **chocolate**
½ pound **margarine**, softened
1 cup fine **sugar**
3 **eggs**, separated
8 whole **matzahs**
Sweet wine
½ cup **nuts**, chopped

Preparation:

Melt chocolate in double boiler. Let **cool. Cream** sugar with margarine until fluffy and sugar is dissolved. **Add** egg yolks, one at a time, and **beat** well. **Beat** egg whites until stiff. **Fold** melted chocolate into egg yolk mixture and **fold** in beaten egg whites. Reserve ½ cup of chocolate mixture to use for frosting the top and sides of finished cake.

Dip each matzah (one at a time) into wine. **Do not** soak too much. **Place** one matzah on a flat tray. **Cover** with a tablespoonful of chocolate filling. **Spread** filling to cover the whole surface of the matzah. **Place** another matzah on top and repeat. **Continue** this process until all matzahs are used up. **Cover** top and sides of finished cake with reserved chocolate frosting.

Decorate top with nuts and cover with plastic wrap. **Leave** in refrigerator **24 hours. Cut** into squares or small pieces.

Divine Chocolate Cake

Ingredients:

4 (1 ounce) squares semisweet **chocolate**, chopped
½ cup unsalted **butter** or **margarine**
¾ cup **sugar**
½ cup **cocoa**
3 **eggs**, beaten
¼ teaspoon **salt**
1 teaspoon **vanilla**

Preparation:

Preheat oven to **300 degrees.** Using solid shortening, **grease** an 8 inch cake pan and **dust** with cocoa; **set** aside.

In microwave, **melt** chocolate and butter or margarine in bowl on medium power, **stirring** once, until melted. **Add** sugar, ½ cup cocoa, eggs, and vanilla and mix well. **Pour** into prepared pan. **Bake** at **300 degrees** for **30 minutes.**

Cool for 5 minutes, then **turn** out onto rack and **cool** completely. **Serve** with melted vanilla or chocolate ice cream, if desired, for a sauce. **Serves 8.**

Lemon Sponge Cake

Ingredients:
12 **eggs**, separated
1½ cups **sugar**
¼ cup **potato flour**
1 cup **matzah meal**
⅔ cup **walnuts**, chopped (optional)
½ cup **orange juice**
Grated rind of 2 **lemons**
Grated rind of 1 **orange**
Pinch of **salt**

Preparation:
Preheat oven to **325 degrees.** Using an electric mixer or food processor, **beat** the egg yolks until **frothy** and lemon colored. Gradually **add** sugar, then orange juice and grated lemon and orange rind. **Add** nuts, if desired. **Sift** potato flour and matzah meal together. **Add** to mixture. **Beat** egg whites until **frothy.** Add a pinch of salt and beat until stiff but not dry. **Fold** into other ingredients.

Bake in an ungreased 10 inch angel food pan for **1 hour.** **Invert** pan and **cool** thoroughly before removing cake. **Serves 8.**

Almond Macaroons

Ingredients:

4 **egg yolks**
1 cup **sugar**
2 cups **almonds**, ground
25 **almonds**, halved (for topping)

Preparation:

Preheat oven to **350 degrees**. Beat egg yolks well; **add** sugar and **beat** until mixture is lemon colored. **Add** ground almonds and **mix** thoroughly. **Chill** for **1 hour** in refrigerator.

Take small pieces of mixture and **shape** into small balls. **Place** macaroons on greased baking sheet. **Top** with half an almond. **Bake** in oven for **10 minutes**. Yields roughly **50** macaroons.

Brownies

Ingredients:

3½-4 ounces bittersweet **chocolate**
¼ cup **margarine** or **butter**
2 **eggs**
⅛ teaspoon **salt**
⅔ cup **sugar**
½ cup **cake meal**
½ cup **nuts**, chopped (optional)

Preparation:

Melt chocolate and margarine over hot water. **Let** cool. **Beat** eggs and salt until thick and lemon colored. Gradually **beat** in sugar, then cooled chocolate mixture. **Add** cake meal and **beat** until well blended. **Stir** in chopped nuts. **Spread** batter in well greased 8x8 inch pan and **bake** at **350 degrees** for **15 minutes**. **Cut** into 2 inch squares while warm.

Variation:

For mocha fudge brownies, **add** 1 - 2 teaspoons instant coffee.

Blondies

Ingredients:
1½ cups **brown sugar**
¼ cup **white sugar**
1 tablespoon **vanilla sugar**
1 cup unsalted **butter** or **margarine**
2 **eggs**
¼ teaspoon **salt**
1 cup **matzah meal**
1 cup **potato starch**
1 cup semisweet **chocolate**, coarsely chopped
1 cup **walnuts** or **pecans**, coarsely chopped

Preparation:
Line an 8x10 inch brownie pan with greased foil. **Cream** brown sugar, white sugar, and vanilla sugar with butter or margarine. **Blend** in eggs. **Stir** in salt, matzah meal, and potato starch. **Fold** in chocolate and nuts. **Chill** for **20 minutes.**

Preheat oven to **350 degrees. Spread** and **press** batter into prepared pan. **Bake** about **35 - 40 minutes,** until the center is just set. **Cut** into squares. Let **cool,** then use foil to lift out squares from pan.

Pineapple Sorbet

Ingredients:

1 medium to large ripe **pineapple**
1¼ cups **sugar**
3 tablespoons fresh **lemon juice**, strained
2 tablespoons **Cognac**

Preparation:

Peel pineapple. **Remove** and **discard** center core. **Cut** pineapple into pieces and **purée** in blender. **Add** remaining ingredients and **pulse**. **Strain** the purée through a mesh sleeve, **pushing** with back of a spoon to obtain as much purée as possible. **Discard** the residue in the strainer. **Place** in freezer until semi-frozen. **Re-beat** until creamy and **freeze** completely.
Yields approximately **3 cups** strained purée.

Fabulous Cheesecake

Ingredients:
¼ cup **matzah meal**
¼ cup **brown sugar**
2 pounds **cream cheese**, softened
4 **eggs**
1¾ cups **sugar**
1 teaspoon **vanilla**
Juice and grated rind of 1 **lemon**

For Topping:
¼ cup **sugar**
¼ cup **water**
10 ounces **apricot preserves**
1 tablespoon **brandy**

Preparation:
   Preheat oven to **325 degrees**. **Butter** a 9 inch springform pan. **Combine** matzah meal and brown sugar and use to **dust** pan. **Mix** remaining ingredients and **beat** for 5 minutes. **Pour** into pan and **place** inside larger, oven safe glass dish containing 2 inches of boiling water. **Bake 1¾ hour** or until top is brown (The cake will rise and crack a little).
   Turn off oven and let cake remain in oven 1 hour longer. **Remove** from oven and **cool** for several hours (the cake will fall slightly). **Run** sharp knife around edge and turn onto serving plate. **Combine** topping ingredients in a saucepan and **simmer** 5 minutes. **Serve** warm with cake. Cheesecake may be frozen without the topping.

Ice Cream Puffs

Ingredients:
½ cup **butter**
1 cup **water**
1 cup **matzah meal**
4 **eggs**
Ice Cream
Chocolate syrup

Preparation:
Butter cookie sheet. **Preheat** oven to **450 degrees**. **Place** butter and water in saucepan and **heat.** When butter is melted, **add** matzah meal all at once. **Stir** vigorously until batter no longer sticks to sides of pan. **Remove** from stove and **cool** for 5 minutes.

Add eggs one at a time, **beating** after each is added. **Place** heaping tablespoons of batter on baking sheet, about 2 inches apart. **Bake** 15 minutes. **Reduce** oven to **325 degrees; continue baking** 10 - 15 minutes more. **Remove** from oven. If puffs don't fall, they're ready; if they do, **bake** a little longer. **Remove** from baking sheets and **cool.**

Cut in half, horizontally. When ready to serve, **warm** chocolate syrup in pan. **Place** each bottom half of puff on dessert plate. **Add** scoop of ice cream, then the other half of puff. **Top** with chocolate syrup. Yields **10 ice cream puffs.**

Index